CW00409999

DEVON LIBRARIES
Please return this book on or before the last date stamped below.
Renew on tel. 0845 155 1001 or at www.devon.gov.uk/libraries

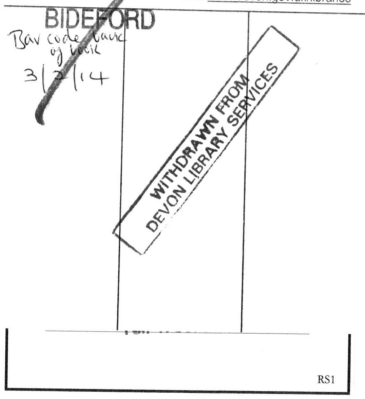

RS1

Francis Frith's

NORTH DEVON
LIVING MEMORIES

photographs of the mid twentieth century

Francis Frith's

NORTH DEVON
LIVING MEMORIES

Dennis Needham

FRITH
BOOK Co

First published in the United Kingdom in 2001 by
Frith Book Company Ltd

Hardback Edition 2001
ISBN 1-85937-261-9

British Library Cataloguing in Publication Data

Francis Frith's North Devon Living Memories
Dennis Needham

Frith Book Company Ltd
Frith's Barn, Teffont,
Salisbury, Wiltshire SP3 5QP
Tel: +44 (0) 1722 716 376
Email: info@frithbook.co.uk
www.frithbook.co.uk

Printed and bound in Great Britain

Front Cover: South Molton, The Square c1955 S362038

Contents

Francis Frith: Victorian Pioneer

FRANCIS FRITH, Victorian founder of the world-famous photographic archive, was a complex and multi-talented man. A devout Quaker and a highly successful Victorian businessman, he was both philosophic by nature and pioneering in outlook.

By 1855 Francis Frith had already established a wholesale grocery business in Liverpool, and sold it for the astonishing sum of £200,000, which is the equivalent today of over £15,000,000. Now a multi-millionaire, he was able to indulge his passion for travel. As a child he had pored over travel books written by early explorers, and his fancy and imagination had been stirred by family holidays to the sublime mountain regions of Wales and Scotland. 'What a land of spirit-stirring and enriching scenes and places!' he had written. He was to return to these scenes of grandeur in later years to 'recapture the thousands of vivid and tender memories', but with a different purpose. Now in his thirties, and captivated by the new science of photography, Frith set out on a series of pioneering journeys to the Nile regions that occupied him from 1856 until 1860.

Intrigue and Adventure

He took with him on his travels a specially-designed wicker carriage that acted as both dark-room and sleeping chamber. These far-flung journeys were packed with intrigue and adventure. In his life story, written when he was sixty-three, Frith tells of being held captive by bandits, and of fighting 'an awful midnight battle to the very point of surrender with a deadly pack of hungry, wild dogs'. Sporting flowing Arab costume, Frith arrived at Akaba by camel seventy years before Lawrence, where he encountered 'desert princes and rival sheikhs, blazing with jewel-hilted swords'.

During these extraordinary adventures he was assiduously exploring the desert regions bordering the Nile and patiently recording the antiquities and peoples with his camera. He was the first photographer to venture beyond the sixth cataract. Africa was still the mysterious 'Dark Continent', and Stanley and Livingstone's historic meeting was a decade into the future. The conditions for picture taking confound belief. He laboured for hours in his wicker dark-room in the sweltering heat of the desert, while the volatile chemicals fizzed dangerously in their trays. Often he was forced to work in remote tombs and caves where conditions were cooler. Back in London he exhibited his photographs and was 'rapturously cheered' by members of the Royal Society. His reputation as a photographer was made overnight. An eminent modern historian has likened their impact on the population of the time to that on our own generation of the first photographs taken on the surface of the moon.

Venture of a Life-Time

Characteristically, Frith quickly spotted the opportunity to create a new business as a specialist publisher of photographs. He lived in an era of immense and sometimes violent change. For the poor in the early part of Victoria's reign work was a drudge and the hours long, and people had precious little free time to enjoy themselves. Most had no transport other than a cart or gig at their disposal, and had not travelled far beyond the

boundaries of their own town or village. However, by the 1870s, the railways had threaded their way across the country, and Bank Holidays and half-day Saturdays had been made obligatory by Act of Parliament. All of a sudden the ordinary working man and his family were able to enjoy days out and see a little more of the world.

With characteristic business acumen, Francis Frith foresaw that these new tourists would enjoy having souvenirs to commemorate their days out. In 1860 he married Mary Ann Rosling and set out with the intention of photographing every city, town and village in Britain. For the next thirty years he travelled the country by train and by pony and trap, producing fine photographs of seaside resorts and beauty spots that were keenly bought by millions of Victorians. These prints were painstakingly pasted into family albums and pored over during the dark nights of winter, rekindling precious memories of summer excursions.

The Rise of Frith & Co

Frith's studio was soon supplying retail shops all over the country. To meet the demand he gathered about him a small team of photographers, and published the work of independent artist-photographers of the calibre of Roger Fenton and Francis Bedford. In order to gain some understanding of the scale of Frith's business one only has to look at the catalogue issued by Frith & Co in 1886: it runs to some 670 pages, listing not only many thousands of views of the British Isles but also many photographs of most European countries,

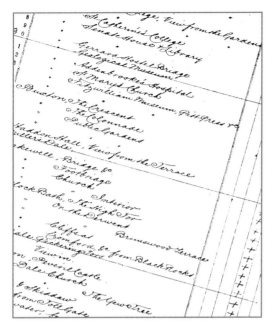

and China, Japan, the USA and Canada – note the sample page shown above from the hand-written *Frith & Co* ledgers detailing pictures taken. By 1890 Frith had created the greatest specialist photographic publishing company in the world, with over 2,000 outlets – more than the combined number that Boots and WH Smith have today! The picture on the right shows the *Frith & Co* display board at Ingleton in the Yorkshire Dales. Beautifully constructed with mahogany frame and gilt inserts, it could display up to a dozen local scenes.

Postcard Bonanza

The ever-popular holiday postcard we know today took many years to develop. In 1870 the Post Office issued the first plain cards, with a pre-printed stamp on one face. In 1894 they allowed other publishers' cards to be sent through the mail with an attached adhesive halfpenny stamp. Demand grew rapidly, and in

1895 a new size of postcard was permitted called the court card, but there was little room for illustration. In 1899, a year after Frith's death, a new card measuring 5.5 x 3.5 inches became the standard format, but it was not until 1902 that the divided back came into being, with address and message on one face and a full-size illustration on the other. *Frith & Co* were in the vanguard of postcard development, and Frith's sons Eustace and Cyril continued their father's monumental task, expanding the number of views offered to the public and recording more and more places in Britain, as the coasts and countryside were opened up to mass travel.

Francis Frith died in 1898 at his villa in Cannes, his great project still growing. The archive he created continued in business for another seventy years. By 1970 it contained over a third of a million pictures of 7,000 cities, towns and villages. The massive photographic record Frith has left to us stands as a living monument to a special and very remarkable man.

Frith's Archive: A Unique Legacy

FRANCIS FRITH'S legacy to us today is of immense significance and value, for the magnificent archive of evocative photographs he created provides a unique record of change in 7,000 cities, towns and villages throughout Britain over a century and more. Frith and his fellow studio photographers revisited locations many times down the years to update their views, compiling for us an enthralling and colourful pageant of British life and character.

We tend to think of Frith's sepia views of Britain as nostalgic, for most of us use them to conjure up memories of places in our own lives with which we have family associations. It often makes us forget that to Francis Frith they were records of daily life as it was actually being lived in the cities, towns and villages of his day. The Victorian age was one of great and often bewildering change for ordinary people, and though the pictures evoke an impression of slower times, life was as busy and hectic as it is today.

We are fortunate that Frith was a photographer of the people, dedicated to recording the minutiae of everyday life. For it is this sheer wealth of visual data, the painstaking chronicle of changes in dress, transport, street layouts, buildings, housing, engineering and landscape that captivates us so much today. His remarkable images offer us a powerful link with the past and with the lives of our ancestors.

Today's Technology

Computers have now made it possible for Frith's many thousands of images to be accessed almost instantly. In the Frith archive today, each photograph is carefully 'digitised' then stored on a CD Rom. Frith archivists can locate a single photograph amongst thousands within seconds. Views can be catalogued and sorted under a variety of categories of place and content to the immediate benefit of researchers.

Inexpensive reference prints can be created for them at the touch of a mouse button, and a wide range of books and other printed materials assembled and published for a wider, more general readership - in the next twelve months over a hundred Frith local history titles will be published! The day-to-day workings of the archive are very different from how they were in Francis Frith's time: imagine the herculean task of sorting through eleven tons of glass negatives as Frith had to do to locate a particular

See Frith at www. frithbook.co.uk

sequence of pictures! Yet the archive still prides itself on maintaining the same high standards of excellence laid down by Francis Frith, including the painstaking cataloguing and indexing of every view.

It is curious to reflect on how the internet now allows researchers in America and elsewhere greater instant access to the archive than Frith himself ever enjoyed. Many thousands of individual views can be called up on screen within seconds on one of the Frith internet sites, enabling people living continents away to revisit the streets of their ancestral home town, or view places in Britain where they have enjoyed holidays. Many overseas researchers welcome the chance to view special theme selections, such as transport, sports, costume and ancient monuments.

We are certain that Francis Frith would have heartily approved of these modern developments in imaging techniques, for he himself was always working at the very limits of Victorian photographic technology.

The Value of the Archive Today

Because of the benefits brought by the computer, Frith's images are increasingly studied by social historians, by researchers into genealogy and ancestory, by architects, town planners, and by teachers and schoolchildren involved in local history projects.

In addition, the archive offers every one of us an opportunity to examine the places where we and our families have lived and worked down the years. Highly successful in Frith's own era, the archive is now, a century and more on, entering a new phase of popularity.

The Past in Tune with the Future

Historians consider the Francis Frith Collection to be of prime national importance. It is the only archive of its kind remaining in private ownership and has been valued at a million pounds. However, this figure is now rapidly increasing as digital technology enables more and more people around the world to enjoy its benefits.

Francis Frith's archive is now housed in an historic timber barn in the beautiful village of Teffont in Wiltshire. Its founder would not recognize the archive office as it is today. In place of the many thousands of dusty boxes containing glass plate negatives and an all-pervading odour of photographic chemicals, there are now ranks of computer screens. He would be amazed to watch his images travelling round the world at unimaginable speeds through network and internet lines.

The archive's future is both bright and exciting. Francis Frith, with his unshakeable belief in making photographs available to the greatest number of people, would undoubtedly approve of what is being done today with his lifetime's work. His photographs, depicting our shared past, are now bringing pleasure and enlightenment to millions around the world a century and more after his death.

North Devon Living Memories
An Introduction

What image does the word 'Devon' instinctively bring to mind? Crowds of noisy holidaymakers wearing silly hats and eating ice cream? Probably. Yet whilst this may well apply to the south, and the Torbay coast in particular, most of the north has escaped these aspersions. North Devon even claims its own identity, so as not to be confused with the effete south.

Lying alongside the rivers Taw and Torridge, North Devon is located roughly to the west of Exmoor and north of Dartmoor. These two natural barriers meant that until the railways pointed their iron fingers towards the area relatively late in the Railway Age, access was difficult and few made the effort to get there. Thus this feeling of being cut off from the rest of the country created an altogether different

culture - until Victorian times, at least.

By the time the railways made their impact on North Devon, the south had enjoyed them for years. The dawning of the age of the paid holiday saw the southern coast resorts ready to absorb the masses. Most of the north was not. This has not altered for most of the 20th century. Where the rest of the country was moving rapidly to the culture of the car and motorways, such luxuries were alien to North Devon. It was not until the 1980s that a decent access road was provided, replacing a twisting narrow old highway that was originally built to handle horse-drawn traffic. Thus the great car-borne invasion of the 1960s and 1970s simply did not happen in North Devon. Motorways were just a new word in the dictionary; even today, there

are less than two miles of dual carriageway throughout the region - and that is subjected to a 50mph speed limit.

All this has created a somewhat insular culture in the area - one that pervades to some degree to this day. It is not difficult to find someone who has never been abroad - or who has never visited London, even. Slow and gentle in both speech and mien, the true Devonian is a delightful person, not yet wholly corrupted by modern life.

For all that, there is plenty of absorbing history. The largest town in the north - there are no cities - is Barnstaple. Athelstan was supposed to have granted a charter to the town in 930, making it the oldest borough in England. Millenary celebrations were held in 1930, which had the effect of setting that date in stone. Many scholars, however, feel that Alfred the Great was instrumental in creating a fort at Pilton to defend against Danish insurgents. Only as a result of this did Barnstaple develop. One point beyond dispute is that Athelstan established coin minting in the town.

Whoever is correct, there was a substantial settlement at the time of Domesday. New charters were granted in 1154 and 1189, and the town continued to grow both in size and importance. Its location close to the estuary - but well sheltered from it - was assuming increasing importance; for several hundred years, Barnstaple's history was one intimately connected with the sea and seafaring. In 1588, the town sent five ships to join Drake in overcoming the Spanish Armada. Commerce was flourishing at this time; but it was not to do so for too much longer. The estuary was already prone to silting, and getting ships to Barnstaple Quay was becoming increasingly difficult. A new quay had been built around 1550, although there was a degree of flood prevention work involved rather than providing extra berthing accommodation for ships. Despite the increasingly difficult passage, freight was still delivered to the town by water well into the 20th century.

One other factor that increased the importance of Barnstaple was that it had a bridge over the river. The Longbridge was already in existence by 1200, its exact construction date being unknown. It seems, unusually for the time, that all the sixteen arches were built of stone. It is also possible that the platform nearest to Barnstaple was built to form a drawbridge. Longbridge was originally constructed as a packhorse bridge with large refuges to allow walkers to escape the horses. Over the centuries, it has been progressively widened and strengthened; its historical significance was confirmed in 1937, when it was classified as an Ancient Monument.

One event that has made Barnstaple famous throughout Devon is its fair. This has been held since time immemorial. It started off as a

celebratory event after the huge annual market which lasted for a week. Horses, other livestock and produce were traded, and farm labourers found new positions here. Today, the livestock market is held every Friday, and the Pannier Market - so called because the original stallholders would bring their produce to market by horse in panniers - is held every Tuesday and Friday. The fair, meanwhile, still takes place, but it is essentially an event within the modern meaning of the word. A large collection of showmen and their rides assemble during September, and the town becomes hyper-active for a few days.

As we said earlier, it was the arrival of the railways that brought the world to North Devon. The railway from Exeter arrived in 1854 at the station which survives to this day. It became known as Barnstaple Junction 20 years later when the line to Ilfracombe was opened. This involved building a spindly iron bridge over the Taw alongside the Longbridge. Immediately on reaching the far side, a station - Barnstaple Quay - was opened. This lasted until 1898, when the narrow gauge railway to Lynton was built. There was no room to bring this line into Quay station, so the station closed; it was re-located a few yards further along the Quay and was re-named Barnstaple Town. Famous trains, including the Devon Belle, crossed the river here, and a direct service to London Waterloo left several times each day. The Town station buildings are still

intact, although the line to Ilfracombe closed in 1970.

The Great Western Railway constructed their line from Taunton into Barnstaple Victoria station in 1873. This brought the iron road across Exmoor, and provided places like South Molton with trains. Other services from Barnstaple Junction station linked the town with Bideford, Torrington and Halwill Junction (for Bude and other Cornish stations). They were progressively closed, with the last service to Bideford running in 1965. Today, the railway is a pale shadow of its former self: a single carriage trundles to Exeter and back, up to seven times each day.

The omnibus was first seen in the town in 1919, when Colwill's started a service to Braunton and Ilfracombe. By 1922, services were so numerous that a new bus station was needed. This was built in the Strand, alongside what was the site of Quay station. As a matter of historic record, this station served the needs of Barnstaple's bus travellers until July 1999, when a new station was opened on Queen's Street.

Ilfracombe is one town that really developed to cope with the influx of holidaymakers. Yet the railway builders faced some fearful hills before they brought the line to town. To the end, engines coughed and worked very hard to conquer the gradients needed to beat the hills. The town was different to all the others in North Devon because a lot of the trade was of the day

tripping variety. Paddle steamers from South Wales crossed the Bristol Channel, frequently disgorging hordes from the steelworks and collieries there onto an unsuspecting town.

Bideford is a most attractive place with huge historic interest. Some of our greatest seafarers were born here and trade with the Americas was early and large. But if Torrington, Holsworth and South Molton are all attractive small market towns, it is the undeveloped and wild countryside and the pretty villages hiding down narrow banked lanes that really define North Devon. This will be graphically revealed within these covers.

What follows is a comprehensive record of life in one of England's more remote corners. You are holding history in your hands. Unlike most standard works on that subject, this book is alive and vibrant. Rather than seeing how this wonderful corner of England looked a century or more ago, you can see it as is was - literally within living memory. You will see scenes that you will remember as a youngster - perhaps you will be able identify yourself (or your parents) in one of the 150 gorgeous illustrations. This is nostalgia pure and simple, designed to bring back your memories.

This volume is divided into five chapters. Within each of these, the pictures are arranged so that, hopping into a car to visit the locations, they will follow more or less sequentially. Study the pictures, and note the way fashions developed rather than changed. Absorb the dozens of small details that are there for the taking. The more you probe, the more you will realise that, although the pace of change has accelerated exponentially within the last forty years up-country, North Devon has evolved gently rather than changed.

Although most of the views in this book were taken within living memory, the era covered was so different. The hustle and bustle of life today, the frenetic pace at which we live - these things would, in those days, be part of some Orwellian nightmare. Who would have conceived, or who would have believed, how complicated life has become.

Yet this is Devon. Locals will tell you that living in this area is one coat warmer and one gear lower that life up-country. That definition, incidentally, seems to apply to anyone who lives beyond the county line. But this is time to escape. So, don't fight it. But whilst you may choose to relax in front of the fire with this volume, it really should inspire you to hit the road for North Devon, to search out these locations and savour them - or even re-acquaint yourself with the area. North Devon is a friendly place to be enjoyed to the full. And, if these wonderful images of a gentler age thrill and delight you, don't forget to say thank you to the Francis Frith Collection for their foresight in carefully husbanding their priceless collection down the years.

The North Coast

Braunton, The Square c1950 B189028
Braunton is the self-styled 'largest village in Devon.'
It is pretty too, as this view indicates. It is much
changed as well: today, the thatched building to
the right has been replaced, Bob Ray's Motorcycle
place is an estate agents, and the road surface has
been slightly improved.

▼ **Braunton, Heanton Street c1950** B189030
The demolished building to the right in photograph No B189028 is on the left here. Heanton Street is substantially unchanged, although the bakery has gone and the bank is now the Nat West. The chequered kerbs are no longer here, and the electricity pole is back away from the roadside and out of reach of errant cars.

▼ **Braunton, Church Street c1950** B189020
Church Street is still narrow, but this idyllic view has gone. The thatched roof is tiled, and mechanical horses line the side of this road, which is now one-way and has had a 20mph speed limit imposed.

▲ **Braunton, West Hill c1955** B189046
We are looking from Church Street across the Caen valley. West Hill has always been a popular corner of Braunton. You will recognise this view immediately; little has changed, save a few new houses in the lower centre, close to the main road.

◄ **Braunton, Caen Street c1955** B189037
This is the centre of Braunton, with the coastal road - Caen Street - ahead. The building on the corner housing a piano tuners is still there, although it has been face-lifted. A mobile phone company currently occupy it. Further along, Lloyds bank, just beyond the Riley car on the right, is still open for business.

Braunton, Caen Street c1960 B189067
This view looks back down Caen Street in the opposite direction to No B189037. Again, Lloyds Bank can be picked out. The view is substantially unaltered, although the businesses have changed hands. The London Inn is now an Usher's house, and the plethora of tobacco adverts has been much reduced in these health-conscious times.

◄ **Saunton**
The Saunton Sands Hotel c1950 S65026
The imposing Saunton Sands Hotel continues to this day, providing an excellent standard of food and accommodation. The beach still gets crowded in summer; the crowds are added to by the development of holiday chalets, which are now located in the immediate foreground just beyond the sand.

Braunton, The Level Crossing and Caen Street c1950 B189018

The Barnstaple to Ilfracombe railway once came through here, but it closed in 1970. The track bed towards Barnstaple is now a cycleway; it is part of the Tarka Trail, a 180-mile footpath around north Devon. The white-painted wall with the hotel name is still in place, but without the name. The building has been converted to a café.

▼ Saunton, The Beach c1950 S65047

A long line of beach huts await the arrival of holidaymakers. They are still here to this day, although should you visit off-season they will not be in place; in winter they are stored behind the sandhills between the beach and the house beyond, sheltered from the Atlantic storms.

◄ Saunton, View from the Sandhills c1950

S65009

Our photographer moved into the sandhills to take this and view No S65062. The house in the centre has been rebuilt, but the small chalet in the foreground exists today. Further chalets have been built to the right-hand side beyond the long low hut.

◄ Croyde, The Beach and the Headland c1960 C200164
This is a typical view of North Devon beaches: generally quiet, always sandy and usually some dramatic scenery within a short distance. This is the beach at Croyde looking towards the headland, which is Baggy Point. Sad to say, in this particular area two large holiday camps disgorge too many visitors at peak times.

◀ **Saunton, The Sands
c1950** S65062
The long lines of breakers visible in this shot show why Saunton Sands have become such a magnet for surfers. Together with Woolacombe Bay (which we will see shortly), beat-up Volkswagen camper vans with boards strapped to the roof are almost ubiquitous in this area today.

▼ **Croyde
The Middleboro Hotel
c1960** C200109
There have been few changes to this view, which is out on the road towards Baggy Point. The abbreviated name has been discarded, and the full 'Middleborough' is now used. A gable has been added over the central upper window, and the drive entrance has been widened and moved. But you can still enjoy a stay at this place.

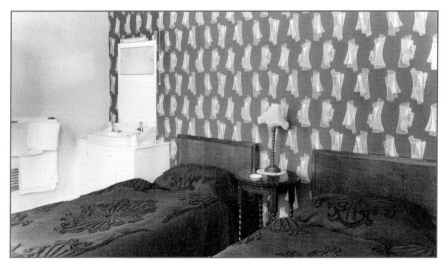

◀ **Croyde
The Middleboro Hotel,
A Bedroom c1960**
C200118
What has changed dramatically, though, is the interior of the hotel. The candlewick bedspreads, garish wallpaper and primitive wash facilities - so typical of that era - are now greatly upgraded. The turned table-lamp is the sort of thing to be discovered in antique shops today.

Croyde, Holiday Motel c1960 C200095
Still substantially unaltered, this building now trades as Atlantis Lodge, and is a guest house. The garden is considerably tidier today. Behind our cameraman are cliffs and the pounding Atlantic ocean.

Croyde, A Flatlet, Holiday Motel c1960 C200108
Today's holidaymaker would swoon if offered such a room now. Then, it was quite acceptable. Cook on the 'Baby Belling' mounted on a stool, sleep in the wartime double bed (probably with a mattress sagging in the middle) and take a bath every Friday ... whether you needed it or not.

Croyde
The Shop, Holiday Motel c1960 C200103
A complete clutter of holiday bits and pieces comprised the
Motel's shop. Note the confectionery just below the sign to the
left. The name of 'Mackintosh' has been lost, first to Rowntree
and then (in 1988) to Nestlé. The box of 'Good News' would
have been a new line then; it was introduced in 1960.

◄ **Georgeham
The Village c1960**
G323031
What a sleepy scene.
You will see an almost
identical one today.
Only the Morris Oxford
and Singer Gazelle cars
have changed. The
King's Arms is still a
glorious little pub,
seldom discovered by
visitors. The
pronunciation of this
village's name is
unusual: the stress is on
the last syllable - almost
making two words.

◄ Georgeham, Putsborough Beach c1960 G323050

Putsborough Beach is to the north of Baggy Point; we are looking towards Woolacombe in the distance. Beyond the house a screen of evergreen trees has been planted and grown; otherwise there has been little change in 40 or more years.

▼ Georgeham The Village c1955

G323004

The rustic charm of this village is easy to see in this view looking towards the heart of the village. In the 1930s, the writer Henry Williamson lived here. His most famous work was 'Tarka the Otter', still loved by youngsters today.

◄ Georgeham Church Street c1960

G323055

We are looking back up Church Street towards the pub. The church gate is on the left. Sad to say, the post office is no more, nor can you sample their Eldorado ice cream. The place is now a private house.

**Woolacombe
General View c1965**
W137116
This is a delightful overview of the resort town of Woolacombe. This has been the most popular resort on this length of coast since the railways first arrived in Victorian times. There was still a station at nearby Morthoe when this view was taken, but judging by the mass of cars in the foreground, it is easy to see why the line closed.

▼ **Woolacombe, The Sands c1955** W137004

Here we see the vast expanse of golden sand that is Woolacombe. The promontory disappearing to the right is Baggy Point, with Croyde beyond. That these sands are good and firm can be seen by the vehicle tracks leading away into the distance.

▼ **Woolacombe, The Beach c1965** W137119

Packed with visitors, the beach at Woolacombe certainly provides a mass of pleasure. Changes in details are all you will see today. The railway in the right-hand corner has gone, and the long building behind has been rebuilt.

▲ **Woolacombe Crazy Golfcourse c1965** W137115

There is plenty of holiday fun to be had on the sea front at Woolacombe. The building in the foreground is still called the Red Barn. It is a restaurant and bar. Behind is the modernistic Narracott Grand Hotel. Today this has expanded further to the right, replacing the building we see here.

◀ **Woolacombe
Beach Road c1965**

W137096

This is Beach Road as it was. Today, the Narracott Grand Hotel - the blank wall to right of centre - has expanded to replace the buildings on the right. Compared with those Victorian beauties, the word 'barracks' is not out of place. A pub on the left is the Golden Hind Tavern.

Woolacombe, Combes Gate c1950 W137007
The narrow road from Woolacombe to Morthoe has this delightful building - The Watersmeet Hotel - en route. The tennis court in front is now a swimming pool; the garages to the right have been demolished, leaving just hard standing for visitors' cars. Behind, the Haven Hotel is now 'Pebbles', and the building higher still is Gull Rock.

◀ **Mortehoe**
The Castle Rock Hotel
c1955 M99012
This fine building was completely flattened at the end of the 1990s. In its place, 13 self-contained flats were built. But by the time it was demolished, the fine hotel had become a nursing home. Its aged residents must have had a wonderful view from their windows.

◀ **Woolacombe**
West Road c1950
W137035
The pretty parade of shops here has been uglified by the tasteless use of colour and plain shop fronts. The large building at the bottom of the road is still the Woolacombe Bay Hotel, and the chemist on the right is still in business, albeit in a new building.

▼ **Mortehoe**
Bull Point Lighthouse c1955 M99003
It is remarkable that this view has altered significantly. It was in 1972 that a large part of the cliff fell into the sea, causing walls to crack and the whole building to be declared unsafe. A temporary lightship was provided by Trinity House until a new building could be constructed. A lighthouse had not been provided here until 1879, although the equipment was modernised in 1960. All this was transferred to the replacement building, which functions to this day. The tiny 1500-watt light in the 35ft tower has wonderfully complex optics that allow it to be seen for 25 miles.

◀ **Lee, The Post Office**
c1955 L27005
This rather grand building offered one of its rooms for a sub-post office. In common with thousands of these places, contemporary economics have seen their purpose largely superseded, and it has closed. There is still a telephone box in place, although it has been replaced by a newer model.

◀ **Lee, Old Maids Cottage c1950** L27050
... which is seen here in a somewhat desolate condition. Such a charming building should not be allowed to fester in this manner. Fortunately when we see it again ...

◀ Lee, The Post Office c1960

L27049

What was the old post office is now the Fuchsia Tea Room, entirely in keeping with the 'olde worlde' nature of the village. Confusingly, the white building ahead is called 'The Old Post Office.' The car on the extreme right is waiting outside Old Maids Cottage ...

▼ Lee
Old Maids Cottage c1960

L27057

... only a few years later, there has been a considerable sum of money spent on the place. The thatch has been renewed, all the creepers have been removed, and even the ugly central chimney stack has gone. Alas, today the pristine white paint is a dirty grey, and the general appearance of the cottage is reverting to the previous view.

◀ Lee, The Bay c1960

L27068

The wild coastline is what draws many visitors to Lee. It is tucked away down at the end of a narrow lane, and is relatively unknown. The locals like it that way, but the village pub and the hotel (pictured here in the centre) cannot make a living without visitors.

Ilfracombe, Mullacott Filling Station and Café c1960 15072
Sad to say, this wonderful art deco filling station has been swept away. A caravan site, pub and restaurant now occupy the space. There are some super views out to sea from here, which is the high point in the climb from sea level in Ilfracombe.

Ilfracombe, The Carlton Hotel c1965 15232
This is one of many elegant hotels built to serve the holiday trade in Ilfracombe. Many have now fallen on hard times, and have seen some changes of use. Not the Carlton. It is still pretty much in the condition we see it in here. Only a small extension to the right-hand end has really changed.

Ilfracombe
The Pavilion and Victoria Gardens c1950 15057
The sea front at Ilfracombe has altered beyond recognition. All the
Victorian and Edwardian development you see here has been
cleared away. Even the large hotel seen to the extreme left has
been replaced by a theatre.

Ilfracombe
Capstone and the Front c1950 15040
Capstone Hill is quite a feature of Ilfracombe.
Covered with paths over the top and around the
seaward side, it is a source of much pleasure to
visitor and resident alike. An ice cream van still
stands on the front in summer. Fortés have been
replaced by Hockings of Appledore, makers of
simply superb ice cream. As mentioned in the next
caption, the Pavilion (the building on the right)
has been demolished.

Ilfracombe, Victoria Promenade c1950 15029
The main building here is the Pavilion. This was damaged by fire in the 1970s and partially restored, but it was finally demolished in the 1990s. Its replacement, the Landmark Theatre, built on the site of the demolished Ilfracombe Hotel, has a controversial exterior - it has been variously described as Madonna's bra or a power station.

Ilfracombe, The Parade, Centre c1950 15031
To take this view of the town, our cameraman gained access to an upstairs room in the Ilfracombe Hotel. That view is no longer possible following the demolition of the building. The parade of shops on the right have elegant wrought iron canopies. The harbour, which we will examine next, lies beyond the church tower.

Ilfracombe
The Harbour c1955
I5118
A varied collection of
craft lie at anchor
behind the sea wall.
This view was taken at
high tide: the water
disappears beyond the
inner wall as the tide
ebbs. The pier to the
right - restored in 2001
- is where the steamer
in view No I5026 is
moored.

▼ **Ilfracombe, The Harbour c1955** 15125
This is a similar view to photograph No 15118, which were both taken from St James Park. The Bristol Channel is visible beyond the row of buildings, which are virtually unchanged today.

▼ **Ilfracombe, St James' Gardens c1950** 15026
The edge of Ilfracombe harbour can be seen in this view. The ship tied up could well be either the 'Bristol Queen' or the 'Cardiff Queen', paddle steamers belonging to P & A Campbell, who brought day visitors to the town from South Wales.

▲ **Hele, Main Road c1955**
H66006
Hele is a pleasant little settlement to the east of Ilfracombe with its own little beach. The parade of shops seen in this picture are still extant, but no longer trading. At the bottom of the hill, the Hele Bay Hotel still carries on business.

◄ **Hele, The Post Office c1965** H66008
Like the shops in view No H66006, Hele post office has closed. The telephone kiosk has moved, and a letter box is located behind the Mk 1 Ford Cortina, alongside the bus stop.

Exmoor & Beyond

Berrynarbor, Sterridge Valley c1960 B73011
Beautiful and remote, the Sterridge valley is a narrow cutting with the river in its lowest point. Only about 5 miles long, the Sterridge drains off the hills above Ilfracombe, passing Berrynarbor on its way to the sea at Watermouth. Note the pony and trap still in use.

▼ Berrynarbor, General View c1960 B73051

Here we see how Berrynarbor sits on the side of the Sterridge valley. In the centre distance is the sea. St Peter's Church is the main landmark. It is mainly a 15th-century building; the sandstone tower is dated 1480.

▼ Berrynarbor, The Village c1955 B73042

The narrow main street through Berrynarbor has the church steps to the right. The white building beyond with a 'Teas' sign in the window is now Miss Muffet's Tea Room. Across the road, the 13th-century Bessemer Thatch Hotel offers a welcome to visitors.

▲ Combe Martin Newberry Beach c1955

C145012

Newberry Beach is the first little cove just to the west of Combe Martin. In picture C145002 dated 1950, you can see the change in the different cafe-type buildings on the beach. The surrounding buildings are unchanged today, but both beach cabins have gone.

Combe Martin Seaside Hill and the Harbour c1955 C145048
With no real harbour in Combe Martin, this is the way boat owners used to take their passengers for a sail in the Bristol Channel. The large rock behind the boat's mast is at the entrance to Newberry Beach.

Combe Martin, Newberry Bathing Beach ▶
c1950 C145002

This is a charming little area, slightly away from the main town but popular with the visitors who stay in Combe Martin. If it has a defect, it is that it faces north. With the cliffs behind, the sunshine there can be a little restricted.

Combe Martin, The Harbour c1965 C145158 ▼

Looking across the town from Lester Point, you can start to get an indication of just how straggly Combe Martin is. Built in a steep-sided valley, there is scant room for lateral building, so the houses just go up the river road. It is well over a mile from the sea to the end of the village. The building in the foreground was the Sea View Hotel then: today, it is the Foc'sle Inn.

▲ **Combe Martin, The Seaside c1960** C145113
The slipway in the village is a gathering point for visitors. The building with the flagpole is the Dolphin Inn. Today, it is much brighter and has had larger windows fitted. By 1960, cars were already becoming a problem.

◄ **Combe Martin, The Seaside c1955** C145069
There has been much redevelopment hereabouts. The recess on the left (where you could once park for 6d, 2.5p) is now a garage forecourt. On the right, the building behind the telephone pole has been rebuilt and moved back to the building line formed by the buildings each side of it.

▼ **Combe Martin, The Pack of Cards Hotel c1950** C145007
This is arguably the most fascinating building in Combe Martin. It was built in 1690 and is Grade 2* Listed. The money for it came from a local squire who had won money at cards. To be true to its name, there are 4 floors (the number of suits in a pack), 13 doors on every floor (the number of cards in a suit), 13 fireplaces, 52 stairs and 52 windows (the number of cards in a pack). Today it is a popular establishment offering 3 real ales, food and accommodation. Staying in this B&B is quite an experience.

▼ **Parracombe, The Church and the Schools c1955** P11003
Christ Church, built in 1878, replaced the much older St Petrock's. It was much closer to the village as well. The stone building to the left of the church is the village school. Parracombe remains an unspoilt village out in the wilds.

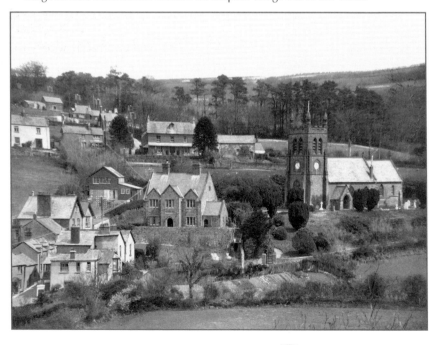

▲ **Parracombe, The Cross Roads and the Hill c1955** P11008
Back in the fifties when this picture was taken, it was not unusual to see a policeman on foot. The village bobby pictured here would have been responsible for law and order all around the Parracombe area. He might not have arrested too many criminals, but his presence was a powerful influence on potentially lawless behaviour.

**◄ Parracombe
The Village c1955** P11024
The village was mentioned in Domesday. It is quite probably the location of the earliest Christian church in Devon. It has changed little in recent years: you can easily locate this particular spot, just up the road from the village pub.

Woody Bay, The Woody Bay Hotel c1955 ▶
W133001
This charming building, in a particularly inaccessible corner of North Devon, still carries on business today, utterly reliant on visitors, so remote is it from civilisation. Long steep hills or a toll road stand between it and revenue-supplying customers. It is a gorgeous spot though.

Brendon, Rockford Village c1955 B194020 ▼
Rockford is only a mile downstream from Brendon. The 17th-century Rockford Inn on the left still sells cider, but it is not advertised on the wall in such a delightful way as it was when this view was taken. The photograph was taken halfway across a footbridge over the East Lyn river.

◀ **Brendon, The Moor and the Village c1955**
B194005
High up on Exmoor, where the East Lyn River flows, this rugged village is popular with visitors, especially as the scenery is so dramatic. A couple of miles further up the valley is Malmsmead, where the legendary Doone family are said to have lived.

▼ **Brendon, The Stag Hunters Inn c1955**
B194002
Again, the East Lyn dominates the scene. Like almost every other corner of the Moor, you will find a village with its own pub. Many of these are relatively un-modified; by their remoteness, they have escaped the dead hand of brewery architects.

◄ **Brendon
The Village c1955**
B194015
Views like this can be
spotted on Exmoor with
relative ease. Things
change but slowly on
Exmoor, one of the last
wildernesses in England.

◄ Brendon
The Village c1955 B194033
Brendon is a straggly village, with houses on either side of the small road that is the villagers' main highway. The most obvious change from this photograph today is the telephone pole. Instead of carrying cross trees with pot insulators, one thick cable delivers the BT service to the village, and it is distributed to the various houses from just the upright.

▼ Stuckeridge
The Black Cat Café
c1950 S811016
In the days before the North Devon Link Road was opened, this was the major route into North Devon. The Black Cat Café was a fuelling stop both for vehicle and driver as this road met the main road from Tiverton to Minehead. The place is still there, although it is on something of a back road now.

◄ Bampton
Castle Street c1950
B379024
Approaching this pleasant little town from Taunton, this was the first view that most drivers got of the place. The view is substantially unaltered today, even if the businesses have changed. Note the old Shell fuel pump on the corner of Staddons.

◀ **Bampton, Fore Street c1955** B379044
As can be seen, this was the old A road to north Devon. Now it is the B3227. The White Horse (to be seen in view No B379013) is just out of shot to the left. You could not mistake this location today.

◄ Bampton
The White Horse Hotel
c1950 B379013

Bampton was once an important stopping-place on the main road from Taunton to the north Devon area; now a new road further south has removed much of the traffic from this place. The pub has lost its porch and the horse above it, but the early 14th-century tower of St Michael's still stands over the town.

▼ Bampton, Fore Street
c1960 B379070

We are a little further along Fore Street from picture No B379044. The chemist to the right is still there today, trading as Bampton Pharmacy. The Standard car on the right would not be seen pointing that way now; today, it is a one-way street, with traffic moving the opposite direction. Ahead is Newton Square.

◄ Bampton
Newton Square c1955
B379029

This view looks back towards Fore Street. Fowlers fish and chip shop is now the village library, and the stone circles on either side of the door are windows now. The White Horse can just be seen on the right.

Bampton, The Railway c1955 B379040
A Great Western class 4575 Prairie (2-6-2 wheel arrangement) loco starts the climb towards Bampton with a train from Tiverton to Morebath Junction. Although overgrown, this view is still available. It was taken at the junction of the A396 and the B3190 by the Exeter Inn, a mile south of Bampton.

Witheridge, Fore Street c1960 W574005
It has been all change here since 1960. On the left, the garage is out of business, but the white building stands, although the garage doors have been infilled. Beyond, everything has been destroyed. Electricity poles still carry supplies to the village. There is a thatcher at work on the right-hand side in the far distance.

Witheridge, Trafalgar Square c1960 W574001
Witheridge is a charming - if straggly - village, as can be seen from this view. The road was once the A373 between Tiverton and South Molton. Now, traffic uses the new A361, and this route has been relegated to the B3137, but still following the same route. In this view, the Hare and Hounds pub to the right is now a private house, and the large electricity pole in the left-hand garden still mars the view. Villages like this are the true heart of Devon, and long may they so remain.

▼ **Witheridge, The Village c1965** W574028
This view is further down the road seen in photograph No W574001. The village shop has gone, as has the second building on the right. Remarkably, the small road sign beyond the car - controlling access to a narrow lane - is still there.

▼ **Witheridge, Trafalgar Square c1950** W574002
We are looking towards the centre of the village; this view is virtually unchanged. A paint job has been done on the house to the right, and the words 'Reed and Sons, Bakers' have been added to the shop, and those are the only changes. St John the Baptist's church in the distance is built of local dunstone.

▲ **Witheridge, The Square c1950** W574018
Two lovely old AEC buses from Devon General await customers in the Square. The shop on the extreme left is still a post office, but the gabled building behind the right-hand bus is no more. On the extreme right is an empty space ...

◄ **Witheridge, The Village c1965** W574031

... that, ten years later, is occupied by a toilet. The centre part of this, a bus shelter then, is now converted to a disabled toilet. Otherwise, this sleepy little village has let the years pass by with little change.

Barnstaple & The Central Belt

Bishops Nympton, General View c1960 B382002
Built on a rise in the ground between the rivers
Mole and Crooked Oak, Bishop's Nympton is a
most attractive village of thatched cottages, with
the 15th-century church dominating all. This is all
set on the very edge of Exmoor.

**South Molton
The Square c1955**

S362038

This was the heart of South Molton - and it still is. The buildings may be unchanged, but their uses have, all except the central one at the far end of the Square. The sign reads: W M Currie, Veterinary & Agric. Supplied, Chemist. Today, still owned by the same family, it is just a chemists. Neither of the coach operators, H J Gardner and Prouts, exist today.

▼ South Molton, The View from Gorton Hill c1955 S362018

This road is the approach to town from the new North Devon Link Road. In the valley is the river Mole. The buildings to the right are part of the town's old industry. A shirt and collar works used to operate from here; now it is an assortment of small engineering businesses. The building in front has been converted to housing.

▼ South Molton, The Square c1955 S362048

The attractive Old Town Hall is to the right; it was built in 1743. The bust above the archway is of Hugh Squier, 'Our Great Benefactor', who died in 1710. The shops in the centre have changed ownership, but the George Hotel is still in business.

▲ South Molton South Street c1955

S362034

Again, little has changed in this view apart from the names on the fasciae. Note the vintage pram outside the newsagents. In the distance on the right, Boots still operate. The tower of St Mary Magdalene's church can be seen beyond.

◀ **Filleigh, The Village c1960** F99011
Before the new road was built, this was the main route between South Molton and Barnstaple, and consequently very busy. Now, it is something of a backwater - and all the better for it. This view is similar today. The right-hand chimney stack and the left-hand cottage have gone. Otherwise, tidied and spruced-up, the view remains.

▼ **Filleigh, Castle Hill c1960** F99012

The ancestral home of the Fortescue family, this house was almost destroyed by fire in 1934 but was rebuilt to its present grandeur. Still in the family today, it is not open to visitors, but can be easily seen from the road where our cameraman did his work.

▼ **Filleigh, The Village c1960** F99010

A wet road and a stream of holiday traffic leaving North Devon: nothing changes. Even this picture is almost as it was then. The addition of a street light just beyond the second ramp is the only real alteration.

▲ **Filleigh, Old Cottages c1960** F99001

This gorgeous row of cottages is no more, deliberately burnt down in the 1960s. But arson it was not. The local fire brigade were looking to practise their technique on thatch fires, and the opportunity to do it here was seized. The local Cine Club were invited along, and several enthusiastic amateur cameramen captured the inferno for posterity. They succeeded in getting in the way, putting themselves in extreme danger and generally having a whale of a time. But the resultant edited film was a triumph, and was used for many years by the fire brigade as a teaching aid.

◄ **North Molton, Fore Street c1960** N60024
On the edge of Exmoor, North Molton is rather a bleak place; it was once a mining village where iron ore was won. This view is largely unaltered, and there is an excellent view of the moors beyond.

◀ **North Molton Court Hall School c1955** N60006
This elegant Jacobean house has always been owned by the Bampfyldes, one of whom was created Lord Poltimore in 1831. The house is still in the distaff side on the family.

◄ North Molton
Fore Street c1955

N60008

Tidying up is all that has happened here in half a century. The grassy bank to the right is now a stone wall, and the building to the right has had its upper storey rendered.

▼ North Molton
The Church c1955

N60016

The building to the extreme right is the old school. War memorial, lych gate and the church itself are unaltered. An unusual aspect of the tower can be seen just below the clock: statues of the Madonna and Child.

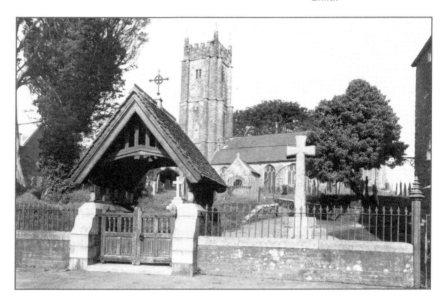

◄ Heasley Mill
The Village c1960

H238014

This charming hamlet is set in the valley of the river Mole. Amazingly for such an apparently peaceful area, mining took place up the valley. Iron and copper were worked, and lead, tin and even silver were found in smaller quantities. Once, a tramway ran through here carrying ore to the railway at South Molton.

◄ **Brayford
The Village c1955**
B387006
Another delightful little
village on the edge of
Exmoor, Brayford has
changed little during the
intervening years. This
view looks south
towards the river Bray;
the village post office is
at the bottom of this hill.

Heasley Mill
Heasley House c1960

H238017
The larger building is the Heasley House Hotel, a most charming establishment and ever-popular with visitors. Note that the house next door has a set of stag's antlers over the door. This is a common adornment of buildings on Exmoor. It does not denote a dead beast; deer shed their antlers every year and grow a new set.

▼ Brayford, The Village from the Bridge c1955

B387007
Brayford boasts a rather splendid Methodist chapel. This can be seen to the right of the picture. An old horse-drawn farm cart stands in the centre behind the pole. The railings on the bridge have been replaced by a wall.

◄ Bratton Fleming
The White Hart Hotel

c1955 B383002
The centre of life in Bratton Fleming, the White Hart has changed over the years. Extended and with an upper storey added to the building on the right, the pub is now a free house - Starkey's ales are but a fond memory.

Bratton Fleming, The Village Street c1955 B383003
This is a typical village of the western edge of Exmoor, although it is outside the National Park. Bratton Fleming is essentially a few houses straggling along either side of a road on a hillside. In this view, the village post office (the low-roofed white-painted building in the centre) still manages to survive. The larger building beyond the car is a Baptist church.

Pilton, The Church and the Old Village c1955 P52008
Higher Raleigh Road gives our photographer the chance to get a good view of the tower of the priory church of St Mary. This was built in 1270, and survived the Dissolution. It was partially demolished during the Civil War to stop the Royalists from using it as an artillery platform; it was rebuilt later.

Pilton
The Street from West Pilton c1940 P52007
This is a timeless scene - almost. The New Inn has become the
Chichester Arms, named after a famous local family (round-the-
world yachtsman Sir Francis was but one of them). Pilton itself is
remarkably ancient; it came into being to defend the bay long
before Barnstaple existed.

◀ **Barnstaple
Rock Park c1950**
B25069
This view was taken from the raised South Walk. Then, as now, it is a popular place for mothers to take their children out in prams (or buggies today). Beyond, Taw Vale Road has changed somewhat since this picture was taken. The Ford garage, Taw Vale Motors, occupies what was Hopgood Haulage Contractors. The old Ford place is now a hotel.

◄ Barnstaple
The River Taw c1950

B25004

Here we see the river Taw upstream of Barnstaple bridge. Pleasure boats lie at anchor, and a steam-hauled freight train heads towards the Junction station where a freight yard used to be located. Today, Barnstaple is the furthest limit of this line, used by passengers only.

▼ Barnstaple
The Embankment from the Park c1950 B25024

It is high tide on the Taw at the sturdy Barnstaple Long Bridge. At the time of this view, locals enjoyed their river. The pontoon to the left was a boathouse where you could hire boats and go for a row. All has now gone.

◄ Barnstaple
The Bus Station c1950

B25023

A lone Southern National service awaits departure time. Railway signals can be seen behind and beyond the single-storied bus station building. This was the Barnstaple Town line off to Ilfracombe. Over the rooftop of the bus is a statue of Queen Anne.

Barnstaple
The Square c1950 B25067
The Square, once the heart of Barnstaple, is seen here from the
roof of Bridge Building. Holy Trinity church tower is prominent,
but look to the left at a conical-shaped roof. This was the pottery
works of Charles Brannam, makers of Royal Barum Ware. Now
demolished, the company operate a modern - and busy - factory
on the edge of town.

Barnstaple, The Fountain and the Clock Tower c1950 B25071
The Prideaux garage remains, although their agency is now Renault and they have moved to the edge of town. Today, the site is occupied by the Bike Shed. The gardens have been converted into an attractively landscaped large traffic island, and the fountain has gone. The Clock Tower and the Imperial Hotel are still there.

Barnstaple, Bear Street and the Post Office c1940 B25008
All has changed here. The inner relief road carved through a decade ago from left to right, destroying the post office and the surrounding houses. The Stag's Head and (partially obscured by the tree) the monumental masons -Youing's - survive on the corner of the new road.

**Barnstaple
High Street c1955**
B25066
The High Street is as
yet not disfigured by
yellow 'No Waiting'
lines on the road
surface. The newly-built
Timothy Whites &
Taylors was hideous
then, as it is today; it is
now a greetings cards
and toy shop. The
white building up the
street on the left is
Martins Bank.

Barnstaple, Bear Street c1940 B25007
From further up Bear Street, we see an indication of what disappeared to allow the new road through. Beyond the bow windows is now mechanised mayhem. The delivery truck parked on the left-hand side is outside the post office. The Ford Popular car seems to want all the road.

Barnstaple, Ebberly Lawn c1950 B25012
We are looking back over the Lawn towards Bear Street. The view is instantly recognisable today. The road is widened a little, and the street furniture has changed. Ebberly Lawn presents a delightful area of green close to the town centre, and is a prized area to live.

The North-Western Coast

Instow, The Lagoon View Caravan Camp, Yelland c1960 I14037
As with a couple of other caravan sites later in this chapter, this one is history. The Taw estuary can be seen beyond the houses, the land mass in the distance is Baggy Point, which we visited in the first chapter.

Instow, The View from the Beach c1955 I14003
This small village at the confluence of the rivers Taw and Torridge offers long expanses of golden sand, but ignores the 'bucket-and-spade' holidaymaker. In 1955, the Jubilee Hall was essentially a shop and tea room. Today, it is a restaurant. The lean-to on the left is rebuilt as a fish restaurant, and the large house to the right is the Decks Restaurant. On the extreme left, the Wayfarer pub serves food. With two more hotels and another pub further along to the right, Instow is the eating-out capital of North Devon.

◄ **Bideford, The Quay c1955** B90057
Buses no longer wait here; their stops are on the road to the left. The Western National service 101 used to operate between Ilfracombe, Barnstaple, Bideford and Westward Ho!. Fishing boats still tie up to the quay, along with the ship that services Lundy Island. On the extreme right, in the distance, note the old lime kilns.

◀ **Instow, The View
from the Beach c1955**
I14004
Taken to the left of
photograph No I14003,
this view shows some of
the old housing in the
village. It is unchanged
to this day. The village
offers a little confusion
to the unwary. Strictly
speaking, this part is
Instow Quay, the hamlet
set back beyond the
reach of winter storms is
Instow Town.

▼ **Bideford
The River and Long Bridge
c1955** B90058
Bideford's famous bridge was
built in 1460; although it has
been widened and improved,
it is essentially the same
structure. With 24 irregularly-
spaced arches and at 677ft
long, it is a real historic
treasure. It was the main A39
road until the late 1980s, when
a new river crossing and
Bideford by-pass was built.

◀ **Bideford
From Chudleigh Fort
c1955** B90054
Chudleigh Fort is on the
south side of the
Torridge at East-the-
Water. This is 16th-
century, and was ruined
for many years. Then it
was acquired by public
subscription and
presented to the town in
1921. It now offers
peace and quiet and a
lovely view over
Bideford - the Little
White Town.

◀ **Northam**
The Approach from
Bay View Road c1955
N37002
This view has greatly
changed following a
road widening scheme.
The war memorial has
moved some 100 yards
to the left, and the road
junction has been re-
aligned. The Church
Hall behind is now a
scout hut.

Bideford, Long Bridge and the Tower c1955

B90048

Here we have a further view of the Long Bridge. The tower in the foreground was built as a folly. It latterly became an apple store; then the greenery was ripped off the walls and it was converted into a rather attractive house.

Northam Bay View Road c1955

N37003

This road is a popular residential area of Bideford, and its very name describes the attraction. It is high on a hill, and there are indeed expansive views out to sea. Poles and trees in this view have altered, but the buildings are pretty well unchanged - although new ones have been built along the left-hand side.

Northam, The Church from the Fields c1955

N37004

The empty field is now housing, appropriately named Glebefields. St Margaret's church is partially 14th-century, and the original vicarage can be seen to the right. The tower here was a landmark for boats out at sea for many centuries.

▼ **Appledore, Marine Parade c1955** A55016
Appledore is a quaint village on the north side of the Torridge. The view here is of the more modern end towards Bideford. The cars are interesting: a Standard Vanguard 'Beetleback' and an MG sports car are the first two. In the distance, across the river, is Instow.

▼ **Appledore, The Quay c1950** A55002
The sea has been Appledore's lifeblood for ever. In this view, a steamer, the 'Strait Fisher' from Barrow, appears to be unloading into barges. The quay itself has been rebuilt and improved over the years. The narrow streets and ancient cottages are a magnet for today's visitor.

▲ **Northam, Westward Ho! from Northam c1960** N37009
This caravan site is but a memory now, as is the track to the right. This was a wartime construction, allowing tanks to cross the boggy Burrows and the Pebble Ridge. Westward Ho! was built as a response to Charles Kingsley's eponymous novel, and became all that was bad about uncontrolled development. Today, slowly, the worst excesses are being removed.

◄ **Westward Ho!, The Gay Sombrero Café, Interior c1960** W71100
This view, the epitome of the period, was repeated a thousand times around the country. Take a theme, install a coffee machine and a few snacks. Then all you have to do is to add a flashy new cash register on the counter, and seating for the poseurs of the day. The effect is almost minimalist. This photograph also indicates how disgracefully we have corrupted that most descriptive word 'gay'.

◀ **Westward Ho! High Seas c1955**
W71064
Another wonderful image of the times. Warm coats seems to be the order of the day - except for the two girls to the right. In those days, young ladies still had to be coy. But they still had the need to display to the fellers that they had developed into women. This is a perfect example.

**Westward Ho!
The Sands c1955**
W71018
With lots of
accommodation and
caravan sites, Westward
Ho! became a popular
holiday destination,
despite the fact that the
only rail service closed
in 1917. In this view, all
the components of an
English holiday - beach
rides, sea and sun - have
come together.

**Westward Ho!
High Seas c1960**
W71071
A Westward Ho!
holiday! The sea
thrashes in at the height
of a storm, the pile of
deck chairs lie,
unwanted, under
tarpaulins and offer
shelter to two girls. A
regular scene in winter,
it is rare to combine
high tides and storms in
this fashion during the
season.

◀ **Westward Ho! The Holiday Centre Chalets** W71025
Westward Ho! (the only place in England with an exclamation mark after its name) has long been the centre for inexpensive holiday accommodation. These - and other - huts have been cleared now; they have been replaced by a luxurious static caravan site, something of an improvement.

◀ Westward Ho!
From Kipling Tors c1955
W71046

The major building in the centre has gone now, and serried ranks of static caravans lie behind. At the top of the beach is Pebble Ridge, a natural phenomenon 2 miles long, 50ft wide and 20ft high. Behind is the famous North Devon golf course. Rudyard Kipling went to school in the town, hence the name of this hill.

▼ Abbotsham
The Village c1955   A3234

Before the road was improved, the village revolved around the major farm. The cottages to the left belonged to that set-up. Now, they farm visitors: the Big Sheep is a major tourist attraction in the area. The chap on the motor cycle could well be of the Dark family. They ran the post office - which was in the white building - for many years.

◀ Bucks Mills
Cottages c1960
B240003

A fissure in the cliffs; this is Bucks Mills. There has been little development here, but the village is loved by locals who despise the commercialism of Clovelly. Cob and thatch cottages such as these are the true picture of Devon, even today.

▼ **Clovelly, Downalong c1960** C124061
Clovelly has been owned by one family for centuries. This explains the complete lack of change. You even have to pay to visit the place. This view shows two aspects of Clovelly that survived until relatively recent times. Donkeys were its prime source of haulage, and the sled was its cart. Here, we see sacks (of coal?) being delivered to a house.

▼ **Clovelly, High Street c1960** C124166
Here we see another sled in use, this time carrying Lassie dog food. The post office (and other businesses here) thrive on the hordes of visitors who find the place irresistible. Unusually by today's norms, the post office still survives.

▲ **Clovelly
Donkey Stealing Sugar
c1960** C124085
Inevitably, the donkeys became quite a feature of Clovelly. In this gorgeous posed shot, the donkey helps herself to the sort of reward expected from visitors. This sort of view would find its way around the world as picture postcards, dispatched by enthusiastic visitors.

◄ **Clovelly**
The Harbour c1960

C124142

The tiny harbour in Clovelly has sent boats to sea from time immemorial. Clovelly herrings have long been a special treat. Now, the shoals are no more. The Red Lion pub is a popular place to stay when visiting. Author Charles Kingsley spent his childhood here - his father was the local vicar.

Hartland, Quay Hotel c1955 H31018
Set on the southern headland where the Bristol Channel becomes the Atlantic Ocean, Hartland has seen its share of shipwrecks over the years. Evidence can still be seen all around. The Quay Hotel is still in business, virtually unchanged from when this view was captured.

Hartland, The Quay c1955 H31024
Sharp rocks stick out from the sea, waiting to claim any boat foolish enough to come close. The cluster of buildings to the right is where the hotel is located, as we saw in view No H31018. The land mass on the skyline is Lundy: the island's name is Norse for Puffin Island.

To The South

Extracts from:
Holsworthy, The New Housing Estate c1950 H161010
Lifton, The Arundell Arms c1950 L195024
Lifton, Fore Street c1950 L195009
Northlew, The Square 1961 N85013

◄ **Holsworthy
The Square c1950**
H161006
All these buildings can
be identified today, even
if they have virtually all
acquired new names on
the fasciae. The
telephone box has been
removed, and the road
surface has been
improved.

◄ Holsworthy
Fore Street c1950
H161004

A small market town, Holsworthy is still as attractive today as it was half a century ago, when these pictures were taken. It is little changed either. Barclays has now acquired a white surface rendering to conceal the previously quite attractive finish. Otherwise, signs and cars notwithstanding, the view is instantly recognisable.

▼ Holsworthy
The White Horse and the Crown and Sceptre Hotels c1950   H161007

The granite tower of St Peter and St Paul's church was built around 1500; the other buildings in this view were built a little later. The elegant curved building is currently a ladies' hairdressers.

◄ Holsworthy
Fore Street c1950
H161019

The Crown and Sceptre is one of the best pubs in town, with a particularly lively landlord. The entrance has been modified somewhat, and the left-hand of the two openings is now a window. Across the road outside the Kings Arms, a very early touring caravan stands and an old Ford car comes lumbering past.

◄ **Lifton**
The Village c1960
L195018
A small village on the western approaches to Dartmoor, Lifton is less than a mile from the Cornish border. The medieval church of St Mary the Virgin is its most outstanding feature. This place existed in Saxon times, and is referred to in King Alfred's will.

◀ Holsworthy
The New Housing
Estate c1950 H161010

Once a feature of life in many parts of the country, the 'pop man' used to deliver soft drinks on a weekly basis. His lorry was always a welcome sight amongst youngsters. Here, Corona is being delivered - the same stuff you can still buy today.

▼ Lifton, The Cottage
Hotel c1950 L195003

This attractive building at the east end of the village is substantially unchanged half a century after our photographer visited. Only the climbing shrub at the far end of the building has been removed.

◀ Lifton
The Arundell Arms
c1950 L195024

In the days when these pictures were taken, Lifton was on the main A30 trunk road to the west, and suffered greatly from holiday traffic. That has all gone now, but it does leave places such as this Pub searching for a new source of business.

◄ **Lifton**
Fore Street c1950 L195009
Two ancient petrol pumps
are the main feature in this
view. Sad to say, the whole
of this courtyard has been
cleared. Behind the pumps
are what appear to be
boxes. These will be oil
dispensing cabinets. In
those far-off days, our cars
sometimes burnt almost as
much oil as they did petrol.
At that time one bought it
loose, by the pint.

◄ Lifton
The Village c1955

Ll95015

A relatively quiet road was available to our photographer when he captured this splendid view of the Arundell Arms. The pub is still completely covered by foliage, and the view is otherwise quite unchanged.

▼ Northlew
The Bridge 1961

N85011

The village stands on a hill overlooking the river Lew, which is (surprise) to the north. In this charming view, the house we can see is unaltered now apart from the porch; the bridge railings, although similar, are housed in more substantial posts.

◄ Northlew
The Square 1961

N85013

This wide Square is still in use today. The Bedford coach - almost the industry standard in the 1950s - waits for its next run. Just to its rear, a cover protects the village well. The other vehicle is a brewer's dray, delivering to the Green Dragon Inn behind. A barn (extreme right) is now converted to a house.

▼ **Northlew, St Thomas of Canterbury Church c1965** N85014
This is an atmospheric view that springs to life when you visit today. The only alterations are cosmetic improvements, although the Ford car has been replaced by a Mini. The flagpole atop the church has been removed.

▼ **Torrington, Taddiport c1955** T64021
Down by the river Torridge, Taddiport used to be a leper colony. In the foreground, housing has replaced the leper fields, and the factory has been extended and re-developed. At the time of this view, it was a creamery, but it now has a variety of uses.

▲ **Torrington Taddiport Bridge c1955**
T64005
Taddiport was a port of sorts - for a few years. The Rolle (or Great Torrington) canal used to link the town with the port of Bideford. This view of the 17th-century bridge is taken from the front of the factory shown in picture No T64021, and is roughly where the canal came through. This disappeared in 1871 when its place was taken by a railway.

◀ **Torrington**
The Waterloo Memorial
c1955 T64009
Overlooking the Torridge
valley, the memorial was
built in memory of that
great battle. Left of centre,
the cluster of buildings is at
Town Mills, where the canal
first ran. To the right of the
road which disappears
towards the top of the
picture is the Royal
Horticultural Society's
gardens at Rosemoor.

◄ **Bishops Tawton
The Village c1960**
B105026
The main Exeter to
Barnstaple road (the
A377) now by-passes
the village centre. This is
the road to the right. To
the left is Village Street,
which leads towards the
Square and the original
heart of Bishops Tawton.
Four decades after our
photographer visited,
there is hardly a change
to be noted.

◄ Torrington
Fore Street c1950
T64015
The attractive Town Hall is the building with an arch, to the right. On its wall today, the citizens of Great Torrington have an ornate clock to tell them the time. Little else has changed over the intervening years.

▼ Bishops Tawton
Hill Rise c1950 B105002
The beautifully-thatched cob cottages are still as attractive, with only a thatched porch over the upper two doors to note as a change today. St John the Baptist church is 14th-century, although it was rebuilt in the 19th.

◄ Bishops Tawton
The Square c1960
B105019
The Square has kerbstones around it, but anyone returning to the village after a long time away would find this view instantly recognisable. The pub on the right is the Chichester Arms, and the family's coat of arms is affixed to the wall.

▼ Bishops Tawton, Mill Cottages c1960 B105016

Another view of Bishops Tawton that shows how little things have changed. A replacement building behind and above the main one is all you will note that is different. Our photographer was standing in a small grassy area that has now been used as a car park.

▼ Swimbridge, General View c1955 S241015

Swimbridge is a small village that used to straddle the main Barnstaple/South Molton road before the new road was built. Now it is a quiet backwater. The factory was a tannery, but it is now converted to residential use. The white-roofed building is the Jubilee Parish Hall.

▲ Swimbridge, The Post Office and the Village c1955 S241002

We are looking towards Barnstaple. The village shop is still in business, although it is not selling Dominion Petrol any longer. Neither are the milk churns collected each day. Note also the metal hoarding advertising Westward Ho Smoking Mixture. The house to the right has been rebuilt, with the building line preserved.

◀ **Swimbridge, The Church and the Bridge c1955**

S241008

This broach spire, 102ft tall, is built in the style of St Peter's, Barnstaple. The church (St James's) is packed with interest. A stone pulpit is 15th-century, as is the beautiful rood screen, which was restored in about 1880. Between 1832 and 1880, the curate here was John (Jack) Russell. He was the hunting parson who bred the terriers which would carry his name.

Landkey, General View c1955 L193002
Here we have an overview of the valley which contains Landkey and Landkey Newland just a little beyond. There is little that can be specifically said to have changed from the time of this picture to the present. This is just glorious Devonian countryside.

Landkey, The Village c1955 L193015
Compared to the surrounding countryside and villages, Landkey is something of an aesthetic disappointment. The old main road came through here, but today most of the traffic is to and from Barnstaple. Landkey has become something of a dormitory village for the town.

Index

Frith Book Co Titles

www.frithbook.co.uk

The Frith Book Company publishes over 100 new titles each year. A selection of those currently available are listed below. For latest catalogue please contact Frith Book Co.

Town Books 96pp, 100 photos. County and Themed Books 128pp, 150 photos (unless specified). All titles hardback laminated case and jacket except those indicated pb (paperback)

Around Aylesbury (pb)	1-85937-227-9	£9.99	Down the Thames	1-85937-121-3	£14.99
Around Bakewell	1-85937-113-2	£12.99	Around Dublin	1-85937-058-6	£12.99
Around Barnstaple	1-85937-084-5	£12.99	Around Dublin (pb)	1-85937-	£9.99
Around Bath	1-85937-097-7	£12.99	East Anglia (pb)	1-85937-265-1	£9.99
Berkshire (pb)	1-85937-191-4	£9.99	East London	1-85937-080-2	£14.99
Around Blackpool	1-85937-049-7	£12.99	East Sussex	1-85937-130-2	£14.99
Around Bognor Regis	1-85937-055-1	£12.99	Around Eastbourne	1-85937-061-6	£12.99
Around Bournemouth	1-85937-067-5	£12.99	Edinburgh (pb)	1-85937-193-0	£8.99
Around Bradford (pb)	1-85937-204-x	£9.99	English Castles	1-85937-078-0	£14.99
Brighton (pb)	1-85937-192-2	£8.99	English Country Houses	1-85937-161-2	£17.99
British Life A Century Ago	1-85937-103-5	£17.99	Around Exeter	1-85937-126-4	£12.99
British Life A Century Ago (pb)	1-85937-213-9	£9.99	Exmoor	1-85937-132-9	£14.99
Buckinghamshire (pb)	1-85937-200-7	£9.99	Around Falmouth	1-85937-066-7	£12.99
Camberley (pb)	1-85937-222-8	£9.99	Folkestone	1-85937-124-8	£9.99
Around Cambridge	1-85937-092-6	£12.99	Gloucestershire	1-85937-102-7	£14.99
Cambridgeshire	1-85937-086-1	£14.99	Around Great Yarmouth	1-85937-085-3	£12.99
Canals and Waterways	1-85937-129-9	£17.99	Greater Manchester (pb)	1-85937-266-x	£9.99
Cardiff (pb)	1-85937-093-4	£9.99	Around Guildford	1-85937-117-5	£12.99
Carmarthenshire	1-85937-216-3	£14.99	Around Harrogate	1-85937-112-4	£12.99
Cheltenham (pb)	1-85937-095-0	£9.99	Hastings & Bexhill (pb)	1-85937-131-0	£9.99
Around Chester	1-85937-090-x	£12.99	Helston (pb)	1-85937-214-7	£9.99
Around Chichester	1-85937-089-6	£12.99	Herefordshire	1-85937-174-4	£14.99
Around Chichester (pb)	1-85937-228-7	£9.99	Around Horsham	1-85937-127-2	£12.99
Churches of Berkshire	1-85937-170-1	£17.99	Humberside	1-85937-215-5	£14.99
Churches of Dorset	1-85937-172-8	£17.99	Around Ipswich	1-85937-133-7	£12.99
Colchester (pb)	1-85937-188-4	£8.99	Ireland (pb)	1-85937-181-7	£9.99
Cornish Coast	1-85937-163-9	£14.99	Isle of Man	1-85937-065-9	£14.99
Cornwall	1-85937-054-3	£14.99	Isle of Wight	1-85937-114-0	£14.99
Cornwall (pb)	1-85937-229-5	£9.99	Kent (pb)	1-85937-189-2	£9.99
Cotswolds (pb)	1-85937-230-9	£9.99	Kent Living Memories	1-85937-125-6	£14.99
County Durham	1-85937-123-x	£14.99	Lancaster, Morecambe & Heysham (pb)		
Cumbria	1-85937-101-9	£14.99		1-85937-233-3	£9.99
Dartmoor	1-85937-145-0	£14.99	Leeds (pb)	1-85937-202-3	£9.99
Derbyshire (pb)	1-85937-196-5	£9.99	Around Leicester	1-85937-073-x	£12.99
Devon	1-85937-052-7	£14.99	Leicestershire (pb)	1-85937-185-x	£9.99
Dorset	1-85937-075-6	£14.99	Around Lincoln	1-85937-111-6	£12.99
Dorset Coast	1-85937-062-4	£14.99	Lincolnshire	1-85937-135-3	£14.99
Dorset Living Memories	1-85937-210-4	£14.99	London (pb)	1-85937-183-3	£9.99
Down the Severn	1-85937-118-3	£14.99	Ludlow (pb)	1-85937-176-0	£9.99

Available from your local bookshop or from the publisher

Frith Book Co Titles (continued)

Around Maidstone	1-85937-056-x	£12.99	South Devon Coast	1-85937-107-8	£14.99
Manchester (pb)	1-85937-198-1	£9.99	South Devon Living Memories	1-85937-168-x	£14.99
Peterborough (pb)	1-85937-219-8	£9.99	Staffordshire (96pp)	1-85937-047-0	£12.99
Piers	1-85937-237-6	£17.99	Stone Circles & Ancient Monuments		
New Forest	1-85937-128-0	£14.99		1-85937-143-4	£17.99
Around Newark	1-85937-105-1	£12.99	Around Stratford upon Avon	1-85937-098-5	£12.99
Around Newquay	1-85937-140-x	£12.99	Suffolk (pb)	1-85937-221-x	£9.99
Norfolk (pb)	1-85937-195-7	£9.99	Surrey (pb)	1-85937-	
North Devon Coast	1-85937-146-9	£14.99	Sussex (pb)	1-85937-184-1	£9.99
North Yorks	1-85937-236-8	£9.99	Swansea (pb)	1-85937-167-1	£9.99
Norwich (pb)	1-85937-194-9	£8.99	Tees Valley & Cleveland	1-85937-211-2	£14.99
Around Nottingham	1-85937-060-8	£12.99	Thanet (pb)	1-85937-116-7	£9.99
Nottinghamshire (pb)	1-85937-187-6	£9.99	Tiverton (pb)	1-85937-178-7	£9.99
Around Oxford	1-85937-096-9	£12.99	Around Torbay	1-85937-063-2	£12.99
Peak District	1-85937-100-0	£14.99	Around Truro	1-85937-147-7	£12.99
Around Penzance	1-85937-069-1	£12.99	Victorian & Edwardian Kent	1-85937-149-3	£14.99
Around Plymouth	1-85937-119-1	£12.99	Victorian & Edwardian Maritime Album		
Norfolk Living Memories	1-85937-217-1	£14.99		1-85937-144-2	£17.99
North Yorks (pb)	1-85937-236-8	£9.99	Victorian and Edwardian Sussex	1-85937-157-4	£14.99
Preston (pb)	1-85937-212-0	£9.99	Victorian & Edwardian Yorkshire	1-85937-154-x	£14.99
Reading (pb)	1-85937-238-4	£9.99	Victorian Seaside	1-85937-159-0	£17.99
Salisbury (pb)	1-85937-239-2	£9.99	Warwickshire (pb)	1-85937-203-1	£9.99
Around St Ives	1-85937-068-3	£12.99	West Midlands	1-85937-109-4	£14.99
Around Scarborough	1-85937-104-3	£12.99	West Sussex	1-85937-148-5	£14.99
Scotland (pb)	1-85937-182-5	£9.99	West Yorkshire (pb)	1-85937-201-5	£9.99
Around Sevenoaks and Tonbridge	1-85937-057-8	£12.99	Weymouth (pb)	1-85937-209-0	£9.99
Somerset	1-85937-153-1	£14.99	Wiltshire Living Memories	1-85937-245-7	£14.99
South Hams	1-85937-220-1	£14.99	Around Winchester	1-85937-139-6	£12.99
Around Southampton	1-85937-088-8	£12.99	Windmills & Watermills	1-85937-242-2	£17.99
Around Southport	1-85937-106-x	£12.99	Worcestershire	1-85937-152-3	£14.99
Around Shrewsbury	1-85937-110-8	£12.99	York (pb)	1-85937-199-x	£9.99
Shropshire	1-85937-083-7	£14.99	Yorkshire Living Memories	1-85937-166-3	£14.99

Frith Book Co titles available 2001

Around Bedford (pb)	1-85937-205-8	£9.99	Lake District (pb)	1-85937-275-9	£9.99
Around Brighton (pb)	1-85937-192-2	£9.99	Liverpool and Merseyside (pb)	1-85937-234-1	£9.99
Buckinghamshire (pb)	1-85937-200-7	£9.99	Around Luton (pb)	1-85937-235-x	£9.99
Cheshire (pb)	1-85937-271-6	£9.99	Northumberland and Tyne & Wear (pb)		
Dorset (pb)	1-85937-269-4	£9.99		1-85937-281-3	£9.99
Devon (pb)	1-85937-297-x	£9.99	Peak District (pb)	1-85937-280-5	£9.99
Down the Thames (pb)	1-85937-278-3	£9.99	Surrey (pb)	1-85937-081-0	£9.99
Heart of Lancashire (pb)	1-85937-197-3	£9.99	Sussex (pb)	1-85937-184-1	£9.99
Hereford (pb)	1-85937-175-2	£9.99			

See Frith books on the internet www.frithbook.co.uk

FRITH PRODUCTS & SERVICES

Francis Frith would doubtless be pleased to know that the pioneering publishing venture he started in 1860 still continues today. A hundred and forty years later, The Francis Frith Collection continues in the same innovative tradition and is now one of the foremost publishers of vintage photographs in the world. Some of the current activities include:

Interior Decoration

Today Frith's photographs can be seen framed and as giant wall murals in thousands of pubs, restaurants, hotels, banks, retail stores and other public buildings throughout the country. In every case they enhance the unique local atmosphere of the places they depict and provide reminders of gentler days in an increasingly busy and frenetic world.

Product Promotions

Frith products are used by many major companies to promote the sales of their own products or to reinforce their own history and heritage. Frith promotions have been used by Hovis bread, Courage beers, Scots Porage Oats, Colman's mustard, Cadbury's foods, Mellow Birds coffee, Dunhill pipe tobacco, Guinness, and Bulmer's Cider.

Genealogy and Family History

As the interest in family history and roots grows world-wide, more and more people are turning to Frith's photographs of Great Britain for images of the towns, villages and streets where their ancestors lived; and, of course, photographs of the churches and chapels where their ancestors were christened, married and buried are an essential part of every genealogy tree and family album.

Frith Products

All Frith photographs are available Framed or just as Mounted Prints and Posters (size 23 x 16 inches). These may be ordered from the address below. From time to time other products - Address Books, Calendars, Table Mats, etc - are available.

The Internet

Already twenty thousand Frith photographs can be viewed and purchased on the internet. By the end of the year 2000 some 60,000 Frith photographs will be available on the internet. The number of sites is constantly expanding, each focussing on different products and services from the Collection.

The main Frith sites are listed below.

www.francisfrith.co.uk

www.frithbook.co.uk

See the complete list of Frith Books at:

www.frithbook.co.uk

This web site is regularly updated with the latest list of publications from the Frith Book Company. If you wish to buy books relating to another part of the country that your local bookshop does not stock, you may purchase on-line.

For further information, trade, or author enquiries please contact us at the address below:
The Francis Frith Collection, Frith's Barn, Teffont, Salisbury, Wiltshire, England SP3 5QP.
Tel: +44 (0)1722 716 376 Fax: +44 (0)1722 716 881 Email: sales@francisfrith.co.uk

---

See Frith books on the internet www.frithbook.co.uk

TO RECEIVE YOUR FREE MOUNTED PRINT

Mounted Print
Overall size 14 x 11 inches

Cut out this Voucher and return it with your remittance for £1.50 to cover postage and handling, to UK addresses. For overseas addresses please include £4.00 post and handling. Choose any photograph included in this book. Your SEPIA print will be A4 in size, and mounted in a cream mount with burgundy rule lines, overall size 14 x 11 inches.

Order additional Mounted Prints at HALF PRICE (only £7.49 each*)

If there are further pictures you would like to order, possibly as gifts for friends and family, purchase them at half price (no additional postage and handling required).

Have your Mounted Prints framed*

For an additional £14.95 per print you can have your chosen Mounted Print framed in an elegant polished wood and gilt moulding, overall size 16 x 13 inches (no additional postage and handling required).

---

* IMPORTANT!
These special prices are only available if ordered using the original voucher on this page (no copies permitted) and at the same time as your free Mounted Print, for delivery to the same address

---

Frith Collectors' Guild

From time to time we publish a magazine of news and stories about Frith photographs and further special offers of Frith products. If you would like 12 months FREE membership, please return this form.

Send completed forms to:
The Francis Frith Collection, Frith's Barn, Teffont, Salisbury, Wiltshire SP3 5QP

Voucher for **FREE** and Reduced Price Frith Prints

Picture no.	Page number	Qty	Mounted @ £7.49	Framed + £14.95	Total Cost
		1	**Free of charge***	£	£
			£7.49	£	£
			£7.49	£	£
			£7.49	£	£
			£7.49	£	£
			£7.49	£	£

Please allow 28 days for delivery   *** Post & handling**   £1.50

Book Title . . . .   **Total Order Cost**   £

Please do not photocopy this voucher. Only the original is valid, so please cut it out and return it to us.

I enclose a cheque / postal order for £ . . . .
made payable to 'The Francis Frith Collection'
OR please debit my Mastercard / Visa / Switch / Amex card
(credit cards please on all overseas orders)

Number . . . .

Issue No(Switch only) . . . . .Valid from (Amex/Switch) . . . .

Expires . . . . Signature . . . .

Name   Mr/Mrs/Ms . . . .

Address . . . .

. . . .

. . . .

. . . . Postcode . . . .

Daytime Tel No . . . .   Valid to 31/12/02

The Francis Frith Collectors' Guild

Please enrol me as a member for 12 months free of charge.

Name   Mr/Mrs/Ms . . . .

Address . . . .

. . . .

. . . .

. . . . Postcode . . . .

Free Print - see overleaf